How To Meditate

Meditation Techniques For Beginners Guide Book

©2014 Colin G Smith
http://AwesomeMindSecrets.com

Copyright 2014

All rights reserved. No part of this book may be reproduced or transmitted to any form by any means electronic or mechanical including photocopying, recording or by any information storage and retrieval system without the written permission of the Publisher except where permitted by law.

Disclaimer

This eBook is for educational purposes only, and is not intended to be a substitute for professional

counselling, therapy or medical treatment. Nothing in this eBook is intended to diagnose or treat any pathology or diseased condition of the mind or body. The author will not be held responsible for any results of reading or applying the information.

Table of Contents

About Colin G Smith	1
What is Meditation?	2
The Etymology of Meditation	2
The History of Meditation	3
The Benefits Of Meditation	3
How is Meditation Different From Relaxation, Thinking, Concentration or Self-Hypnosis?	5
Debunking The Myths About Meditation	7
Common Questions About Meditation	9
Q. What are the different styles of meditation?	9
Q. How do I quiet the mind?	9
Q. What is the Best Time of Day to Meditate?	9
Q. Should I Meditate With my Eyes Open or Closed?	10
Q. How Long Should my Meditation Sessions Last?	10
Q. Should I Sit Crossed Legged?	10
Q. When I meditate I experience physical pain in my body. What should I do?	11
Q. Can People Get By Without a Teacher?	11
Basic Brain Science	12
The Benefits of Knowing Your Brainwaves	12
What are Brainwaves?	12
One of the Simplest Ways to Relax Yourself Before Meditating	15
Meditation Techniques	16
Basic Breathing Meditation	16
Part Of You Is Relaxed Now…	16
White Light In / Black Smoke Out	17
Mantra Meditation	17
Infinite Space Heart Chakra Meditation	18
Tonglen	19
Taking & Giving (Tonglen) Meditation in 3 Steps	20
How Do I Know That I Am Meditating Well?	22
Getting The Best Results From Your Meditation Practice	24
Meditation Best Practice Check List:	24
Transcending the Egotistical World	25

About Colin G Smith

For over ten years now I have been driven to find the very best methods for creating effective personal change. If you are anything like me, you're probably interested in simple and straight-forward explanations. Practical stuff that gets results! I am a NLP Master Practitioner, writer & author who has written several books including:

- Boost Your Mind Power: 99+ Awesome Mind Power Techniques
- EFT Tapping: How To Relieve Stress And Re-Energise Rapidly Using The Emotional Freedom Technique
- Neuro-Linguistic Programming NLP Techniques - Quick Start Guide

Visit My Amazon Author Page

What is Meditation?

Meditation is a discipline wherein an individual becomes the master of his mind and modes of consciousness. The reason behind an individual to practice meditation varies. Most of the time, meditation is done to realise a certain benefit.

The term meditation alone is a very broad practice, much like sports, wherein it includes a myriad of techniques and different purposes. More often than not, it is used to promote relaxation and build and strengthen internal energy or life force. At the same time, the practitioner develops compassion, patience, love, forgiveness and concentration which are essential to healthy living.

The Etymology of Meditation

The term meditation has a plethora of meanings in varied contexts. However according to meditation history, its English name was derived from "meditatio" in the Latin language, which is directly connected to the verb "meditari" meaning "to contemplate, ponder, devise or think". According to international sources of the history of meditation, there are also terms related to meditation in the Hebrew Bible, Old Testament, and Tibetan Language. More often than not, they are related to getting familiar with the self through thinking and incorporating within the self virtues such as compassion, concentration, understanding, humility, perseverance and patience.

> *"We are what we think. All that we are arises with our thoughts. With our thoughts, we make the world."* - Buddha

The History of Meditation

The history of meditation is predominantly related with religious contexts in which it is frequently practiced during the ancient times. In the prehistoric times, meditation had already been practiced through rhythmic, repetitive chants to appease their gods. Most scholars who researched meditation history found that the emergence of meditation is accounted to the last stage of human evolution where there was an imminent need to focus the mind.

Some historians reveal that the earliest written references to meditation were found in the writings of Hindu Vegas. It is said that they meditate to connect further with Savitri, their divine god, who is believed to influence their daily life. The history of meditation also expands to China through Taoists and India with Buddhists. The use of meditation dates back to 5th and 6th centuries BCE. Buddhists see meditation as a way to salvation.

It was only during the 20 BCE when meditation was first recorded by Philo of Alexandria. It was found that meditation was used to exercise spiritual activities through prime concentration. By the 3rd century, the practice of meditation was further developed by Plotinus. In Islamic countries during the 8th and 9th century, the custom of Dikhr involved the repetition of names of God which was a form of concentration for worshippers.

The Benefits Of Meditation

Meditation has many specific benefits. People meditate for various reasons. Some meditate for spiritual purposes while some do it for health benefits, some love the art and science of meditation while some simply check it out for a while as a new pastime.

Relaxation

One of the first benefits of meditation is relaxation. Meditation calms the body and relaxes the mind. If you meditate successfully, then you will be at ease with yourself. Your mind will be relieved of stress, you will not be anxious and you won't be affected as much by the many stresses and strains of the real world.

Enlightenment

Meditation can help you to cut yourself off from the busyness of the world but it is by no means escapism or a route to get away from reality. On the contrary, meditation helps you to get enlightened. The hackneyed perception of enlightenment may be hyped and enlightenment doesn't always imply spiritual awakening or connecting with the all-that-is. Meditation can help improve your understanding about yourself and the world. Through meditation, you will be able to connect to your other-than-conscious mind, discover what you truly want, and what you should really be doing in life. Meditation can help you to better understand relationships, love, responsibilities and roles, along with all the other facets of life.

Health Benefits

Meditation has numerous health benefits. To begin with, meditation helps in regulating blood pressure and also enhances blood circulation to the various parts of the body. Proper breathing techniques, the right posture of the body and a calm unflinching mind will help in better blood circulation and will also contribute to improved metabolism. Meditation also helps to hone an active mind and to know if there is something wrong with your physical and psychological self.

Positive Energy

Meditation can help you to be more energetic. It allows you to focus on one thing at a time. It will prevent your mind from tossing from one subject to another or from one thing to another. You will be able to concentrate with increased focus on precisely one task or aspect of life and you will be able to channel all your positive energy towards that thought and to the subsequent accomplishing of that objective.

Improved Memory

Meditation can improve your memory and can also prevent loss of memory or Alzheimer's. Meditation can help you to recollect things faster and it can certainly increase your capacity to think, to reason and improve your cognitive and analytical skills.

How is Meditation Different From Relaxation, Thinking, Concentration or Self-Hypnosis?

Meditation induces relaxation, improves thinking, enhances concentration and has many similarities with self-hypnosis. Yet, meditation is different from relaxation, thinking, concentration and self-hypnosis.

Meditation is often considered to be a form of exercise or an act which leads to a relaxed mind. Mediation is actually a practice and there are various parts and subparts of this practice. Meditation is not just about trying to calm down, relax, to get relief from stress and anxiety, to increase concentration and to improve the ability to think.

Here is a brief guide to help you understand how meditation is different from the other four:

Meditation and relaxation are only interrelated as far as one of the outcomes of meditation being relaxation is concerned. When someone meditates successfully, one can attain relaxation. But relaxation can be mental or physical. Relaxation by the virtue of lying on the couch is physical. Relaxation by the virtue of reading a good book is primarily mental or psychological. Relaxation by the virtue of meditation is both physical and psychological and in addition to that it is spiritual as well.

Meditation and thinking are very different. Thinking is a purely mental exercise and when you think, your body plays an important role. Where you are, what you are doing, how comfortable you are or not, how stressed or anxious you are, how many external factors have a direct or indirect impact on your ability to think and your own cognitive and analytical skills will determine the nature, scope and outcome of your thinking. While meditating, most of these factors will not come into play. You will be cut off from the external world, you will be calm, relaxed and relieved from stress and anxiety and you shall be able to think lucidly and with definite purpose. Also, meditation improves your cognitive and analytical skills due to clarity of thought, something general thinking or casual thinking may not be able to achieve.

Meditation and concentration are related in the same way as meditation and relaxation. One of the benefits of meditation is concentration but the vice versa doesn't happen. Concentration can be attained without having the mind and body working in unison or being in harmony. But concentration by the virtue of relaxation is achieved by inducing harmony of the body, mind and soul.

Meditation and self hypnosis are similar in many ways but there are differences as well. One key difference is that the former involves the mind, body and soul while the latter involves only the mind and doesn't have much to do with the body or the soul.

Debunking The Myths About Meditation

Meditation can be an excellent recreational activity and may even help lead to a higher sense of well-being, depending on the person. It has been practiced for centuries by the lowliest of peasants and the most important of nobles alike. Today, people from all different walks of life practice meditation and many people are quickly jumping onboard to experience the wonders and amazing effects meditation can have on the body and mind.

Unfortunately, there are a lot of meditation myths floating about the Internet and the market. Many sites and businesses claim to sell products 'absolutely necessary' for meditative relaxation. Other sources talk about having the one-and-only way to properly meditate and 'experience a higher form of meditation'. Many of these myths about meditation are useless and even harmful to the meditation experience. Many of the myths below are commonly propagated on the Internet and by questionable businesses.

Meditation Requires Certain Products, Paraphernalia and Purchasable Techniques

One of the many meditation myths on the Internet is propelled by sites that offer things like special crystals or meditation music. Many make claims that meditation 'cannot be successfully achieved' without them. This is one of the most harmful myths about meditation and most of these sites are scams. Meditation is for the most part, a relaxation of the mind and body. You can do this without purchasing expensive products. There are some products and techniques available on the market for helping with the process, but there is no such thing as a 'meditation necessity'.

Meditation Requires Being Part of a Certain Religion

Another one of the myths about meditation is the idea that one must be Buddhist, Hindu or some other kind of religion in order to meditate. While these religions do often practice meditation, there is no religious requirement to meditate. You have the absolute right to enjoy and appreciate a quiet meditation without converting to a religion. Meditation is something which can be and should be enjoyed by everyone. These meditation myths deserve the boot.

Meditation Requires Body Transcendence and Visions

Hollywood has done an excellent job in creating one of the biggest myths about meditation. Anyone who has seen a movie with meditation sees the meditating individual travelling into the clouds through astral projection or blowing out candles with his mind. However, the meditation myths on body transcendence are over exaggerated. You don't need to have a wild experience in order to meditate. For the most part, the best parts of meditation are experienced after it is done – the relaxation and mental focus to mention some.

Meditation is a beautiful and pure form of mental and physical relaxation. However, one should look more carefully into what meditation is truly about if they don't want to get caught up in pointless meditation myths. Meditation can be a wonderful activity with a wide plethora of personal benefits for you, but the myths about meditation won't help you one bit.

"Meditation is the dissolution of thoughts in Eternal awareness or Pure consciousness without objectification, knowing without thinking, merging finitude in infinity." - Voltaire

Common Questions About Meditation

Q. What are the different styles of meditation?

There are six fundamental styles of meditation:
- Mindfulness Meditation
- Guided Visualisations
- Guided Meditation
- Breathing Exercises
- Mantras
- Music Enhanced Meditation
- Movement Based Meditation

There are thousands of different meditation systems, old and new, but they all incorporate one or more of these methods in their practice.

Q. How do I quiet the mind?

Thoughts are constantly running through our mind even while we sleep. The idea of having no-thoughts is nice but it is not the objective of meditation. You can learn to watch your thought stream without becoming involved or attached to the thoughts and this helps to quieten your mind; That's how meditation can help you.

Q. What is the Best Time of Day to Meditate?

Traditionally Yogis of the ancient world would meditate early in the morning. It's considered a more spiritually pure time for meditating. On a more practical level it is of course a more peaceful time before everyone starts getting up and off to work. The other advantage of early morning meditation is that you can transfer some of the state of mind you generate into your normal daily life at the beginning of the day. Of course many people have very busy lives so the fact is, it's best to fit in a meditation session when it suits you.

Q. Should I Meditate With my Eyes Open or Closed?

This is really down to your own personal experience. Different traditions of meditation say one way is better than the other but it's best to find out what works for you. It can be useful to start off by staring at a candle or a point on the wall before closing your eyes.

Q. How Long Should my Meditation Sessions Last?

When you're first starting out it's good to stick to just 10 to 15 minutes per session. After you have become used to entering meditative states of consciousness you can increase the session times to 20 to 30 minutes. Practicing a regular meditation session, once or twice per day, helps condition your mind and creates a good habit pattern, making it easier to maintain over the long term.

Q. Should I Sit Crossed Legged?

According to Yogic teachings there are advantages to sitting crossed legged or in the lotus position. However not everyone can do it due to body pain. So the main thing when meditating is to sit up with a straight back. It's acceptable to sit on a chair with a cushion to support your back too.

Q. When I meditate I experience physical pain in my body. What should I do?

If your body is unhealthy it will make it difficult for you to sit in one position for a long period of time. Doing Yoga stretching exercises can help your body become more supple and strong. It's a good idea to go for a walk before meditating or try jumping up and down on a mini trampoline/re-bounder for ten minutes. Of course if you start feeling pain during meditation, get up and shake about or walk about a bit to find out if the pain eases off.

Q. Can People Get By Without a Teacher?

You can certainly learn to meditate without a teacher learning from books and ultimately from your own experience which is the real teacher anyway. However it can be useful to be in a class with a qualified teacher because you will experience the energy of group meditation and learn by example from an authentic teacher.

Basic Brain Science

Understanding how your brain works can contribute to your body's functionality in its day to day activities. More often than not, people focus their attention on comprehending emotions so they can function better. However in more recent years research has provided us with a better understanding of brainwave function and the subconscious mind. Being able to control your brainwaves enables you to control many aspects of your being rather than just emotions. It's been observed many times that spiritually inclined individuals, such as meditators and healers, can exercise a greater level of control over their brainwaves.

The Benefits of Knowing Your Brainwaves

As mentioned previously, spiritually inclined individuals can fully influence their body's functions because of their deep understanding of the five brain frequencies: Alpha, Beta, Theta, Delta, and Gamma. Once mastered and fully grasped, an individual can reach deeper states of consciousness and have full control on their outlook in life. Contrary to common belief, reality is not made up of external factors and surroundings. Rather, it is directly influenced by a person's mindset, thoughts, and beliefs. With this being said, an individual has full control of reality by mastering the five different brainwaves.

What are Brainwaves?

Mastering the five different brain frequencies can open the subconscious mind and go into deeper states of consciousness. But what exactly are brainwaves? Brainwaves or brain frequencies are a representation of specific levels of brain activity. Each type has its own unique set of characteristics and requires different approaches for one to take full control of it. A brain frequency is measured by cycles per second or Hertz(Hz.) There are five known brain frequencies:

Beta (14 - 40 Hz)

Beta has 14-40 cycles per second. It is also called the reasoning wave or waking consciousness. These brainwaves are generally related to the normal awakened state of consciousness. The individual is in its fully alert state, critical and logical reasoning. Whilst Beta is effective for normal functioning it also translates to anxiety, restlessness, and stress. Beta is characterised by a small inner critic inside a person's head. Most of the time, adults operate only at the Beta which is why they are usually highly stressed.

Alpha (7.5 - 14 Hz)

This brainwave is also called the deep relaxation wave. It's a state of consciousness usually occurring during light meditation or a simple daydream. Alpha brainwaves can heighten the mind's programming such as visualisation, learning, imagination, memory, and concentration. Alpha is also called the gateway to the subconscious and an individual can get closer to this state of consciousness as the Hertz drops to 7.5. Certain meditation techniques enable you to achieve 7.5 Hz and go into deep relaxation even during awakened consciousness.

Theta (4 - 7.5 Hz)

It is mainly experienced during the REM stage of sleep which is usually experienced momentarily. Experts say one can achieve in-depth spiritual connections and universal union during theta. Unlike other brainwaves, theta is a silent voice. You are still conscious about your environment, however, your body is in deep relaxation.

Delta (0.5 - 4 Hz)

Delta brain frequency is experienced when one is in deep dreamless sleep and in very deep transcendental meditation. It is an important healing process, and it is the gateway to the collective unconscious and universal mind.

Gamma (above 40 Hz)

Recently, brainwave experts discovered the fastest brain frequency at 40 Hz. It is the brain frequency associated with creative inspiration and high level information processing. In spite of this, little is known about this wave and the states of consciousness related to it.

> *"You yourself, as much as anybody in the entire universe, deserve your love and affection."* - Buddha

One of the Simplest Ways to Relax Yourself Before Meditating

There's not much point trying to meditate if you are in an agitated state. To get the best results from your meditation practice it's best to get as relaxed as possible before actually sitting down and meditating. There are some simple and proven methods to relaxing your body and lowering your brainwaves to get yourself into an optimum state for meditation. One of the simplest and direct approaches comes from the world of Yoga. The Corpse Posture is a straightforward exercise that uses your body and the pull of earth's gravity to deeply relax the body and mind.

The Corpse Posture

1. Lay down on the floor on your back.

2. Spread your legs and arms out to your sides so you are kind of like a star fish.

3. Adjust your arms and legs until you are in the most comfortable position.

4. Now simply breath and relax, enjoying the pull of earth's gravity.

5. Do this for a few minutes until you feel more relaxed and ready to sit up for meditation.

Meditation Techniques

The following three meditations are basic relaxation meditations that will enable you to relax body and mind and begin to lower your brainwaves so you can start to access deeper levels of consciousness. These practices are good for daily stress relief and as a preliminary before the more advanced meditations that will allow you to enter deeper levels of mind.

Basic Breathing Meditation

Meditating on the breath is probably the most widely used and ancient of practices for relaxing the mind. It's very effective.

1. Sit down with your back straight.

2. Close your eyes and simply breath through your nostrils and out through your mouth.

3. Just observe the breath going in and out.

4. Try pausing for a second before the out breath, focussing on the heart centre.

Repeat for 10 minutes or more if you can!

Part Of You Is Relaxed Now…

Even if you suffer from aches and pains like many people do, you can always find some part of the body that feels relaxed. By focusing your attention on this feeling you can begin to spread the relaxation throughout your being.

1. Close your eyes and become aware of where the most
1. relaxed part of your body is?
2. Imagine spreading this feeling throughout your body, from the top of your head to the tip of your toes.
3. Enjoy cycling through these relaxing feelings by starting again at step 1.

White Light In / Black Smoke Out

This meditation is a great one to practice. You imagine you are breathing in pure white healing light on the in-breath. On the out-breath you imagine letting out all your stress with black smoke. You can imagine it dissolving into the atmosphere.

1. With your eyes closed, sitting comfortably, imagine breathing in pure white light. Pause.
2. And now imagine black smoking (*stress*) leaving your body on the out breath.
3. Do several rounds of this and notice yourself relaxing more.

With the meditations that follow it is best to practice them when you have done the basic relaxation meditations above so that you're already in a relaxed state of mind and body. When you practice these meditations you will begin to get a sense of your *Essential Self*. This is your true nature. **Pure Consciousness - Infinite Potential!**

Mantra Meditation

The word Mantra is a Sanskrit word meaning; Sacred utterance, numinous sound, or a syllable, word, phonemes, or group of words believed by some to have psychological and spiritual power. Mantra may or may not be syntactic or have literal meaning; the spiritual value of mantra comes when it is audible, visible, or present in thought.

There are many Mantra's you can use. Probably the most well known and ancient Mantra is "*Aum*" or "*Om*." It means The Infinite or The Absolute.

"*Om Mani Padme Hum*" is a very well known Mantra that originate in Tibetan Buddhism. It's usually translated as, "*Hail to the Jewel in the Lotus.*" The jewel in this case is the Buddha of Compassion at your heart centre.

"*I love you, I'm sorry, Please forgive me, Thank You.*" This is a Mantra/Affirmation that comes from the Hawaiian Shamanism System known as Huna. It's known as Ho'oponopono.

1. When you've got yourself into a nice, relaxed and centred space from doing basic breathing meditation you can proceed to recite a mantra.

2. Choose your Mantra of choice and simply begin repeating it in your mind. You can of course say it out loud as well if you prefer.

3. Simply keep repeating the Mantra and notice your experience.

Infinite Space Heart Chakra Meditation

1. Sit down, close your eyes, breath deeply, relaxing more…

    Notice the space between your eyes from behind your eyes.

Notice the space between your ears from behind your ears.

Notice the space between your elbows from behind your elbows.

Notice the space between your knees from behind your knees.

Notice the space between your ankles from behind your ankles.

2. Focus attention on your Heart Centre. Imagine the whole world/Universe dissolving into white shimmering rainbow light. Imagine your body dissolving from the top of your head into your heart and then dissolve your body from the bottom of your feet upwards into your heart.

3. You are now pure Consciousness. Imagine being pure white rainbow light emitting light rays outwards from this Heart Centre into Infinite Space.

NOTE: As you get more used to focussing and becoming one with this heart centre you'll find it easier to find the sweet spot, giving rise to greater feelings of love, oneness and even a little taste of bliss! This location in the Heart Chakra is known as the Indestructible Drop in Tantric Meditation Practice.

Tonglen

Tonglen Meditation, which means *Taking & Giving* in Tibetan, is a special healing practice with an emphasis on the breath. Tonglen Meditation enables a person to TAKE in the *negative* aspects or energies of life, transform this energy into a useful purpose (*destroying one's selfish ego*) and then GIVE OUT positive healing energy. It's useful to know that this practice was kept secret for hundreds of years by advanced Yogis and Teachers because it is so powerful.

> *"Whatever you fight, you strengthen, and what you resist, persists."*
> - Eckhart Tolle

Like most westerners, when I first came across Tonglen I thought it a bit odd! Most western psychological models are still based on getting rid of things that are wrong or bad. The thing is problems you try to run away from or *shove under the carpet* tend to persist. With Tonglen practice we accept the *negative energy*, take it on and indeed harness the energy for transformation! It's a very beautiful way for dealing with your own problematic feelings. Personally I have found Tonglen useful for shifting unwanted states of mind where other approaches / techniques didn't work.

Taking & Giving (Tonglen) Meditation in 3 Steps

1. TAKING: Begin by representing whatever you feel is negative as black smoke. Simply imagine, sense or pretend that there is a cloud of black smoke in front of you. Begin to inhale this cloud of black smoke through your nostrils. Imagine the smoke entering into your body and settling at the area of your heart chakra. Pause your breath there for a moment as you allow that energy to destroy *the demon of demons* – your *self cherishing demon* or ego!

2. GIVING: Now slowly and gently exhale pure white wisdom light through your mouth. You could if you wish imagine beautiful rays of white light and nectars radiating from your body. You are giving away all that is pure, coming from deep within your infinite potential: Your Indestructible Buddha Nature! As you exhale imagine the white wisdom light is

blessing every living being, bestowing peace and happiness!

3. **REJOICING:** As you're exhaling allow yourself to feel joy at practicing giving peace and happiness to others. Pause for a moment at the end of the breath and indulge in it!

REPEAT: You now simply go back and start the taking & giving cycle again.

I highly recommend you practice this outside on a starry evening, it helps you to really expand your consciousness. As you practice the meditation you start to become one with the flow of the breath and you will find yourself melting into the white light. As your brainwaves go deeper down you will begin to feel more and more connected to your *Essential Self*; All that is and ever was.

How Do I Know That I Am Meditating Well?

Almost every person wonders at some point in time if they're meditating well. The first few weeks or months of meditation would be the most uncertain. You may not feel any differences or you may not note the differences that you might be experiencing. Some people are lucky and they get to know if they are meditating well. Most people though need some help to know for sure if they are practising it right.

Here are some signs that will tell you that you are meditating well:

If you are completely at ease with yourself while meditating, then you have made a wonderful start. If you are not at ease then something needs correcting. You may be indulging in a posture that is not ideal or accurate. You may be uncomfortable in that posture in which case you must rectify it. You may not be breathing correctly which will hinder the efficacy of meditation. So shift your posture until you are more comfortable and adjust your breathing until you feel more at ease.

Are you conscious of your entire body and mind? This is one of the most sure-fire signs that you are meditating well. If you can feel different parts of your body and how they react to your breathing and heartbeats, if you can experience calmness in your mind and increased concentration while you are relaxed, then you are meditating well. You may fail to achieve these if you have distractions around you and if you are not in the ideal place that is needed for meditation.

Changes to your lifestyle, nature, mood and your physical self will indicate if you are meditating well:

- *Are you happier than you were?*

- *Have you developed more compassion?*

- *Are you more patient with yourself and others than you were before starting meditation?*

- *Do you look at the world and all material as well as immaterial pleasures in a different way?*

- *Do you know better what you want from life and are able to work towards your goal with renewed zeal and vigour?*

If you answer these questions affirmatively then your meditation is going well. Otherwise you need to look at specifics where you may be going wrong.

Getting The Best Results From Your Meditation Practice

To get the most benefit from meditation you need to practice regularly, daily if possible. Even if you just did ten minutes of basic breathing meditation every day, it would benefit your health and well-being. It's a great way of reducing the daily stress of life. Getting into a routine is the best way to maintain a regular practice. So set a time aside when you can devote ten or twenty minutes of your day to meditation practice.

Meditation Best Practice Check List:

- Pick a time when you will be least likely to be interrupted.
- Are you in a safe, quiet and comfortable place? (Use earplugs if necessary)
- Turn off all phones and gadgetry
- Have a glass of water and blanket near by
- Are you sitting comfortably with a straight back?
- Notice which is most relaxing; Eye's closed or eye's open
- Begin by noticing the flow of air through your nostrils/mouth
- Allow yourself to relax more as you begin one of the basic breathing meditations

Transcending the Egotistical World

We're living in a very ego orientated world. Most of the things we do are based on our ego-identities; Work Roles, Family Roles, Community Roles and even Spiritual Roles. Many of our actions are aimed at acquiring material objects.

Now there is nothing particularly wrong with this. We need to function in the real world but by becoming more familiar with our true nature, our Essential Self, we can remember who and what we truly are: **Pure Consciousness!**

As we become more familiar with this sense of our true nature we will find ourselves becoming more content, peaceful and confident.

> *"Thousands of candles can be lighted from a single candle, and the life of the candle will not be shortened. Happiness never decreases by being shared."* - Buddha

Printed in Great Britain
by Amazon